Penguins

Illustrated by René Mettler
Written by Gallimard Jeunesse
and René Mettler

A FIRST DISCOVERY BOOK

SCHOLASTIC INC. Cartwheel B·O·O·K·S ®

New York   Toronto   London   Auckland   Sydney
Mexico City   New Delhi   Hong Kong   Buenos Aires

Antarctica, at the South Pole,
is the coldest place on earth.
Temperatures can drop to -76°F!
But there are some animals who
don't mind the cold.

Seals

Sperm whales

Killer whale

Penguins

This part of the world is inhabited
by many birds, including penguins.

Albatross

Snow petrel

Southern
giant petrel

Penguins have
webbed feet and short wings.
They cannot fly, but they are excellent swimmers!

All penguins live in the Southern Hemisphere.
Some live in Antarctica, and others live in Australia,
New Zealand, South Africa, and the Galápagos
Islands off the coast of Ecuador in South America.

Emperor penguin

King penguin

Adélie penguin   Gentoo penguin   Chinstrap penguin

Here are three kinds of birds that were once
called penguins, but they are not related to penguins.
They live in the Northern Hemisphere,
and they can fly.

Razorbill

Common murre

Atlantic puffin

Macaroni
penguin

Rockhopper
penguin

Magellanic
penguin

Yellow-eyed
penguin

Fairy
penguin

During mating season, Adélie penguins gather by the hundreds onshore in breeding places called rookeries.

A male Adélie penguin builds a nest out of small stones. Then he looks for a mate. Both the males and females take turns keeping their eggs warm until they hatch.

Emperor penguins have different mating habits. They gather in rookeries on the frozen sea and they do not build nests.

After the female lays the egg, she passes it to the male without letting it touch the ice.

He keeps the egg warm by balancing it on his feet and tucking it under a fold of skin on his stomach.

For about nine weeks, the female goes out to sea to look for food while the male penguin watches over the egg.

During this time, males do not eat at all.
To stay warm in the glacial cold of winter, they
huddle close together and protect their eggs.

From time to time, the penguins on the inside switch with the penguins on the outside who have their backs facing the wind.

There's a surprise
waiting for the
mother penguin
when she returns...
her baby has
hatched!

Penguin mates find each other
amidst the hundreds of other penguins
by recognizing each other's voices.

The mother penguin now
has enough food to feed
her baby. It's the father's
turn to go fish.

About two months after hatching,
young Adélie penguins can look
after themselves. But they have to
watch out for skuas.

The skua is a predatory bird that often attacks small penguins.

Once they are grown, Adélie
penguins spend most of their lives
on ice and in the sea. They only
return to land when it's time
to hatch new penguin chicks.

These are Adélie penguins.
They are very playful.
They love to slide into the
water on their stomachs!

But they have to watch out!
Enemies like this leopard seal
hunt penguins for food!

Penguins look similar to these
marine mammals. They have layers
of fat on their bodies, just like these
mammals do, to keep warm in the
icy cold waters. Penguins spend
much of the time in the water
hunting for fish and sea life to eat.

Weddell seal

Ross seal

Crabeater seal

Killer whale